BOOK ANALYSIS

By Jule Lenzen

The Prime of Miss Jean Brodie
by Muriel Spark

Bright
≡Summaries.com

MURIEL SPARK

SCOTTISH POET AND NOVELIST

- **Born in Edinburgh, Scotland in 1918.**
- **Died in Florence, Italy in 2006.**
- **Notable works:**
  - *The Ballad of Peckham Rye* (1960), novel
  - *The Girls of Slender Means* (1963), novel
  - *Curriculum Vitae* (1992), autobiography

Dame Muriel Sarah Spark (née Camberg) led a highly international and adventurous life. She was born to Jewish parents as the second of two children. Having spent her childhood and youth in Edinburgh and Watford, she moved to Southern Rhodesia at the age of 19 to marry Sydney Oswald Spark in 1937. After the birth of their first and only child in 1938, the marriage had already broken down as Sydney was unstable and abusive. Muriel left her son at a boarding school in South Africa and returned to London in 1944. She had various affairs before converting to Catholicism in 1954. When *The Prime of Miss Jean Brodie* brought her international fame, she spent half her time in New York between 1962 and 65. In 1965, Spark moved to Rome, where she met the Italian sculptor Penelope Jardine. They became close friends and shared a household until Spark's death from cancer in 2006 in Florence. Her son Robin was left out of her will, as they had a troubled relationship during her lifetime. Spark wrote 22 novels, as well as various short stories, essays and biographies. She was well-known and received numerous honours during her lifetime, including a damehood in 1993, eight honorary doctorates and various literature prizes. Her writing is characterised by an experimental style and a theological mindset, and particularly in her writing from 1965 onwards, defined by her many travels.

THE PRIME OF MISS JEAN BRODIE

AN EDINBURGH TALE ABOUT THE INFLUENCE OF A CHARISMATIC TEACHER

- **Genre:** novel
- **Reference edition:** Spark, M. (2000) *The Prime of Miss Jean Brodie*. London: Penguin Books.
- **1st edition:** 1961
- **Themes:** Edinburgh, betrayal, female development, sexual awakening, teaching, fascism, Calvinism, Catholicism

Muriel Spark wrote this novel when she was living in London, and it was to bring her worldwide fame. It is "her sixth and most famous novel" (Stannard, 2011: 2). Christina Kay, Muriel's junior school teacher, served as a model for the charismatic Miss Brodie (*ibid*.). The novel is set in Edinburgh, the capital of Scotland, in the 1930s. In the context of this novel, it is important to note how Stannard defines her writing style: "Always experimental, Spark might be considered the first British post-modernist. At the same time she was a theological (rather than a religious or proselytizing) writer." (*ibid*.: 4)

SUMMARY

The Prime of Miss Jean Brodie is set in Edinburgh and revolves around a teacher at the Marcia Blaine School for Girls, Miss Brodie, a woman in her prime, and her group of protégés: Sandy Stranger, Jenny Gray, Mary Macgregor, Eunice Gardiner, Rose Stanley, and Monica Douglas.

Even though the narrative begins when the girls are 16, it follows them from the age of ten into adulthood. Miss Brodie teaches them during their time at junior school, after which they go on to senior school. Miss Brodie's influence on them does not cease, however, and the girls are referred to as the Brodie set: their education has been so different from that of the other girls at the school that they are immediately recognisable.

JUNIOR SCHOOL

Miss Brodie's approach to teaching is unique: she believes in bringing out the knowledge in the girls, rather than filling them with knowledge on, in her opinion, useless subjects. She tells them the story of her life and love affairs, and introduces them to her personal views: she is a strong supporter of fascism, but also gives the girls a sound education in classical art, and in music. Miss Mackay, the headmistress, disapproves of Miss Brodie's methods but cannot prove anything against her. To this end, she frequently questions the Brodie set but only succeeds after these have left school already.

Miss Brodie takes her set on frequent outings, even after their time in junior school: they go to the theatre, for walks through Edinburgh, and on one occasion even see the ballet dancer Anna Pavlova.

THE BRODIE SET

The reader gets most insight into Sandy's thoughts: she is very imaginative and, rather than seeing or listening to what is going on around her, she daydreams about conversations with characters from novels or people who have impressed her, such as a young policewoman. Sandy goes to a convent, becomes Sister Helena and writes a book on psychology, 'The Transfiguration of the Commonplace'. Jenny is Sandy's best friend during their early school years, and she becomes an actress after school. As children, Jenny and Sandy spend a lot of their free time thinking about Miss Brodie and making up stories about her and her various love affairs. Monica is a mathematician prone to angry outbursts, and later marries a scientist. Eunice is very keen on sports, and always does somersaults and the splits at Miss Brodie's Saturday gatherings. She later becomes a nurse and marries a doctor. She also visits Miss Brodie's grave as an adult. Finally, Rose is 'famous for sex' without having done anything to achieve this fame, and shortly after school marries a successful businessman. Mary is Miss Brodie's scapegoat and later dies in a hotel fire at the age of 24, which leads to feelings of guilt on the part of the rest of the Brodie set and Miss Brodie herself.

MISS BRODIE'S LOVE AFFAIRS

When the girls are 12, Monica observes Miss Brodie and the art teacher, Teddy Lloyd, kissing in the art classroom. However, he is married and Miss Brodie breaks off the affair with him. She enters into another affair with Gordon Lowther, the music teacher, but it is made clear that he is only a consolation, and that Lloyd is her 'true love'. It is the year that the girls are most obsessed with sex, and they make up various theories on Miss Brodie's affairs. Later, when the girls are 15 and 16, Rose poses for Mr Lloyd's pictures, and the girls visit him every weekend in pairs, while they also spend each Sunday with Miss Brodie in Mr Lowther's house in Cramond (Edinburgh). When Mr Lowther marries the science teacher Miss Lockhart, Miss Brodie becomes obsessed with her plan to make Rose Mr Lloyd's lover. Miss Brodie confides in Sandy, and Sandy is the one who betrays Miss Brodie in the end to Miss Mackay. However, it is not Rose who starts the love affair with Mr Lloyd, but Sandy. Mr Lowther once kissed her against her will when she was 15, but at the age of 17 she becomes deeply interested in his infatuation with Miss Brodie and embarks on an affair with him. Miss Brodie seems to be disappointed with the outcome of her plans but resigned to the result. Sandy decides to put a stop to Miss Brodie and hints to Miss Mackay that Miss Brodie teaches the children in her care to support fascism. Miss Brodie is forced to resign and told that it was one of her set who betrayed her, but she only suspects Sandy a few weeks before her own death.

CHARACTER STUDY

JEAN BRODIE

Miss Jean Brodie describes herself as a woman in her prime (p. 10). She feels very strongly about teaching: she feels it is her vocation to dedicate her influence in the best time of her life to the education of young girls, telling her students "You must all grow up to be dedicated women as I have dedicated myself to you." (p. 63). She has strong opinions on various subjects and knows her own mind. She says: "'[...] Give me a girl at an impressionable age and she is mine for life. [...]'" (p. 9). Her views on education distinguish her from the rest of the staff:

> "The word education comes from the root e from ex, out, and duco, I lead. It means a leading out. To me education is a leading out of what is already there in the pupil's soul. To Miss Mackay it is putting in of something that is not there, and that is not what I call education, I call it intrusion [...]" (p. 36).

She is a very independent woman with a dark Roman profile (p. 9), and does not mind what other people say about her. The girls say of her powerful appearance: "[...] she was the square on the hypotenuse of a right-angled triangle, while they [the Kerr sisters] were only the squares on the other two sides" (p. 87).

She is very manipulative and convincing in her guiding of the girls, for example when she tries to set up an affair between Rose and Mr Lloyd:

> "[...] Miss Brodie was [...] spending as much time as possible with Rose and Sandy discussing art, [...] and the necessity for Rose to realize the power she had within her, it was a gift and she an exception to all the rules, she was the exception that proved the rule. Miss Brodie was too cautious to be more precise and Rose only half-guessed at Miss Brodie's meaning, [...]" (p. 110)

She is equally manipulative and commanding in her relationship with Mr Lowther, where she tries to fatten him up (p. 92), as well as taking care of his household.

Miss Brodie is an agnostic and despises the Catholic church. She is a strong supporter of fascism (p. 31). However, she is charismatic and impresses the young girls in her care: "And Miss Brodie was always a figure of glamourous activity even in the eyes of the non-Brodie girls" (p. 112). Even after the Brodie set has left school, they agree that "[...] she was really an exciting woman as a woman. Her eyes flashed, her nose arched proudly, her hair was still brown, and coiled matriarchally at the nape of her neck" (p. 116). Interestingly, Miss Brodie is described as "an Edinburgh spinster of the deepest dye" (p. 26), making this characterisation exemplary of all Edinburgh spinsters of the time.

In the end, Miss Brodie changes. She is forced to retire in 1939 (p. 125) and after that is preoccupied with the question of who betrayed her. Jenny rules that "Miss Brodie is past her prime" (p. 127). Miss Brodie dies just after the war (p. 27).

TEDDY LLOYD

Teddy Lloyd is the art teacher at the Marcia Blaine School for Girls for the senior school. He is a one-armed war veteran and a Catholic. He is married to Deirdre, with whom he has a large family: "The Lloyds were Catholics and so were made to have a lot of children by force." (p. 102). He lives in North Edinburgh, where he also has an art studio (p. 91).

He is unfaithful to his wife, first having an affair with Miss Brodie and later with the 17-year old Sandy. A sense of danger surrounds him, and there are hints of a paedophilic and abusive nature as he forcefully kisses Sandy against her will when she is 15. However, he is infatuated with Miss Brodie, and every single portrait he draws resembles her (p. 120).

SANDY STRANGER

Sandy is frequently characterised by her very small eyes, with which she unnerves other people (p. 107). Even though the reader gets a great deal of insight into her thoughts, she remains an opaque character.

In her early school years, she is close friends with Jenny, and they combine their imaginations in dreaming up stories on Miss Brodie and writing them into a notebook. Sandy herself has a great deal of imagination and spends the majority of her time daydreaming. As she gets older, Sandy becomes increasingly cynical and detached from the Brodie set. She begins to see through Miss Brodie:

> "In this oblique way, she began to sense what went to the makings of Miss Brodie who had elected herself to grace in so particular a way and with more exotic suicidal enchantment than if she had simply taken to drink like other spinsters who couldn't stand it anymore" (p. 109).

Sandy feels superior to Miss Brodie: "[...] she never felt more affection for her [Miss Brodie] in her later years than when she thought upon Miss Brodie as silly" (p. 111). Sandy disdains her: "She thinks she is Providence, thought Sandy, she thinks she is the God of Calvin, she sees the beginning and the end." (p. 120). Sandy betrays Miss Brodie to Miss Mackay shortly after she has graduated from school, in order to put a stop to her (p. 125). However, when asked about the greatest influence of her childhood, Sandy states that it was Miss Brodie (p. 128). Sandy has an interest in psychology (p. 120) and in Calvinism (p. 108). At the age of 17, Sandy has a love affair with the much older, married art teacher Mr Lowther. The fact that he is a Catholic prompts an interest in Catholicism in Sandy and ultimately leads to Sandy's going to a convent. She becomes Sister Helena and writes book on psychology titled 'The Transfiguration of the Commonplace' (p. 35).

ANALYSIS

HISTORICAL AND LITERARY CONTEXT

Religion plays a major role in this novel and various denominations are referred to. Most prominently, Calvinism is mentioned. Sandy describes it as "[...] some quality of life that was peculiar to Edinburgh and nowhere else [...]" (p. 108):

> "In fact, it was the religion of Calvin of which Sandy felt herself deprived, or rather a specified recognition of it. She desired this birthright; something definite to reject. It pervaded the place in proportion as it was unacknowledged. [...]" (pp. 108-109)

Calvinism was advanced in the 16th century by John Calvin, a Protestant reformer, and spread as far as Scotland and the North American colonies (Bouwsma, "Calvinism": n.p.). While Calvinism in many ways resembles the Lutheran Church, Calvin differed from Luther in various points: He saw the World as God's work and still in God's hands, and the presence of Christ in the Holy Communion only in a spiritual sense. He was also a firm believer in predestination, meaning the salvation by God of those worthy. Like Luther, he believed in the original sin. (Bouwsma, "John Calvin": n.p.)

Miss Brodie, by contrast, is an agnostic, and has much to say about the various denominations that the children are confronted with in their daily lives in Edinburgh. For example, on John Knox, the founder of the Presbyterian Church of Scotland, she comments: "[...] 'John Knox, [...] was an embittered man. He could never be at ease with the gay French Queen. We of Edinburgh owe a lot to the French. We are Europeans.'" (p. 33).

She rejects the idea of Girl Guides and Brownies (p. 31) and despises the Catholic religion (p. 85):

> "She always went to church on Sunday mornings, she had a rota of different denominations and sects which included the Free Churches of Scotland, the Established Church of Scotland, the Methodist and the Episcopalian churches and any other church outside the Roman Catholic pale which she might discover." (p. 85)

The novel is set in the 1930s in Edinburgh. This was a time that was characterised by the rise of fascism in various European countries: Mussolini in Italy, and Hitler in Germany. Miss Brodie pronounces herself a supporter and even admirer of both. She even convinces one of her students, Joyce Emily Hammond, to travel to Spain to fight for the fascists (p. 124). The girl dies when her train is attacked.

When the girls are still taught by Miss Brodie, she frequently reads them poetry, "[...] to raise their minds before they went home." (p. 21). One of these poems is 'The Lady of Shallot' by Alfred Tennyson (*ibid*.). Forward says of the poem: "To a degree, then, the isolated Lady in the tower reflects the concept of purity: a passive, cloistered woman would be safe from unchaste behaviour." (Forward, 2014: n.p.). In her reading of James Hogg's poem 'Bonnie Kilmeny', Miss Brodie also underlines the purity of Kilmeny (p. 38). These allusions stand in stark contrast to the stories she tells the girls about her love life.

Other literary works that are mentioned include *Jane Eyre*, which is a strong work on female independence and stands in contrast to the poems Miss Brodie reads to the girls. Miss Brodie also reads a poem by the Scottish poet Robert Burns to them (p. 47), which serves to underline the Edinburgh setting of the novel.

NARRATIVE STRUCTURE

The narrative frequently hints at events that are yet to happen. Its structure is circular: the beginning and the end of the novel are exactly identical. It starts and ends with Miss Brodie calling her set for help against Miss Mackay, and the passage from the beginning of the novel is reproduced word for word at the end: "'[...] Give me a girl at an impressionable age and she is mine for life. [...]'" (p. 9, p. 112). The same structure applies to Sandy, as Sister Helena is visited by a man who asks her about the influences of her childhood, and she replies with "'There was a Miss Jean Brodie in her prime.'" (p. 128), similar to the statement she makes on p. 35 where the same situation is related.

Stannard connects this peculiar narrative structure to Spark's theological attitude to writing:

> "Time is elastic in her fiction, plunging backwards and forwards through analepsis and prolepsis, rendering the narrative present fragile and illusory. There is mankind's time and God's time. The two overlap and interweave." (Stannard, 2011: 4)

The narrative is connected by certain themes which are repeated, one of these being the attributes of the girls, such as Rose being famous for sex (p. 7). Another theme is the girls and the way they wear their panama hats (pp. 6-7). This is referred to again later, when Mr Lloyd does a portrait of the Brodie set in their panama hats (p. 111). Finally, the topic of Miss Brodie's betrayal plays an ongoing role throughout the novel: who was it and what happened? The reader first learns that Sandy betrayed Miss Brodie fairly early on in the novel (p. 60). However, what exactly happened is not revealed until the very last chapter.

IMAGES OF THE DOUBLE IN *THE PRIME OF MISS JEAN BRODIE*

> "For, like very much Scots writing, this is a book preoccupied with the long, old theme of doubleness, of twinship, of each light casting its

> shadow. For antecedent, Dame Muriel has given Miss Brodie the name of the great Deacon Brodie [...]." (McWilliam, 2000: v)

Deacon Brodie is a famous character from Edinburgh. He lived at the same time as the Stevensons and was a cabinet-maker and deacon by day, but a burglar by night. In choosing his last name for her character, Spark hints at the doubleness of Miss Brodie's character: she poses as a virtuous woman in her prime, while at the same time being a fascist and conducting various love affairs.

Several pairs of attributes underline the 'twinship' that McWilliam refers to, for example: "'Do you know, Sandy dear, all my ambitions are for you and Rose. You have got insight, perhaps not quite spiritual, but you're a deep one, and Rose has got instinct, Rose has got instinct'" (p. 107). This twin pair of insight and instinct crops up frequently after this passage has taken place. Interestingly, Miss Brodie says: "'I ought to know, because my prime has brought me instinct and insight, both'" (p. 108). Like her name, her character is defined by doubleness. She also rejects the idea of team spirit, while at the same time being a strong supporter of fascism, a political notion that is based on unity.

What McWilliam refers to as 'twinship' or 'each light casting its shadow' can also be seen in the juxtaposition of the characters of Sandy and Miss Brodie. Sandy grew up under the frequent influence of Miss Brodie, but is also the one to lead to her downfall: the shadow cast by Miss Brodie's light. This juxtaposition is taken even further by setting Sandy's religion against Miss Brodie's politics. The fact that Sandy triumphs further underlines what Stannard has termed as Spark's theological approach to writing.

Finally, doubleness in the novel is also expressed in terms of nationality: "Sandy was sometimes embarrassed by her mother being English and calling her 'darling', not like the other mothers of Edinburgh who said 'dear'." (p. 18). Sandy's last name, 'Stranger', underlines this notion of foreignness.

FURTHER REFLECTION

SOME QUESTIONS TO THINK ABOUT...

- With regard to the theological side of Spark's writing, Stannard states: "A sense of evil, both terrifying and playful, haunts all her writing." (p. 5). Do you think this is true for *The Prime of Miss Jean Brodie*? Where can this evil be found?

- Miss Brodie, as well as other women in the novel, are characterised as having a prime in their lives, a time at which they are at their best. However, the men do not seem to have such a period in their lives. What does this say about gender stereotypes and relations in the novel?

- In the 1969 film adaption, it is not Monica who discovers Miss Brodie and Mr Lloyd kissing, but Mary, who is seen by the two. Why do you think this change has been made?

- Why do you think Sandy renames herself as Sister Helena when she goes to the convent?

- Why do you think Sandy has an affair with Mr Lowther? Is it to prove Miss Brodie wrong or is there some other motivation?

- "She [Sandy] thought of Miss Brodie eight years ago sitting under the elm tree telling her first simple love story and wondered to what extent it was Miss Brodie who had developed complications throughout the years, and to what extent it was her own conception of Miss Brodie that had changed." (p. 120) What do you think? Discuss.
- "The word education comes from the root e fom *ex*, out, and *duco*, I lead. It means a leading out. To me education is a leading out of what is already there in the pupil's soul. To Miss Mackay it is putting in of something that is not there, and that is not what I call education, I call it intrusion [...]" (p. 36). Given Miss Brodie's style of teaching and the way she imposes her own worldviews on her pupils, do you think her own above statement on her teaching methods holds true?
- Why do you think Sandy wants to put a stop to Miss Brodie? Is she worried about her influence on future generations or is it a sense of personal rivalry that prompts this action? Explain your answer.

We want to hear from you!
Leave a comment on your online library
and share your favourite books on social media!

FURTHER READING

REFERENCE EDITION

- Spark, M. (2000) *The Prime of Miss Jean Brodie*. London: Penguin Books.

REFERENCE STUDIES

- Bouwsma, W. J. (2018) Calvinism. *Encyclopaedia Britannica*. [Online]. [Accessed 14 January 2019]. Available from: <https://www.britannica.com/topic/Calvinism>

- Bouwsma, W. J. (2018) John Calvin. *Encyclopaedia Britannica*. [Online]. [Accessed 18 January 2019]. Available from: <https://www.britannica.com/biography/John-Calvin>

- Forward, S. (2014) An Introduction to 'The Lady of Shalott'. *The British Library*. [Online]. [Accessed 14 January 2019]. Available from: <https://www.bl.uk/romantics-and-victorians/articles/an-introduction-to-the-lady-of-shalott>

- McWilliam, C. (2000) Introduction. In Spark, M. *The Prime of Miss Jean Brodie*. London: Penguin Books.

- Stannard, M. (2011) Spark [née Camberg], Dame Muriel Sarah. *Oxford DNB*. [Online]. [Accessed 13 January 2019]. Available from: <https://doi.org/10.1093/ref:odnb/97159>

ADDITIONAL SOURCES

- Gardiner, M. & Maley, W. (2010) *The Edinburgh Companion to Muriel Spark*. Edinburgh: Edinburgh University Press.

ADAPTATIONS

- *The Prime of Miss Jean Brodie*. (1966) [Play]. London: Wydham Theatre.

- *The Prime of Miss Jean Brodie*. (1968) [Play]. New York City: Helen Hayes Theatre.

- *The Prime of Miss Jean Brodie*. (1969) [Film]. Ronald Neame. Dir. UK: 20th Century Fox.

- *The Prime of Miss Jean Brodie*. (1978) [TV series]. UK: Scottish Television Enterprises.

www.brightsummaries.com

Ebook EAN: 9782808017084

Paperback EAN: 9782808017091

Legal Deposit: D/2019/12603/21

Cover: © Primento

Digital conception by Primento, the digital partner of
publishers.

Printed in Great Britain
by Amazon

46457284R00031